101 STORY STARTERS

for Little kids

by

Maisy Day

batchofbooks.com

ISBN: 9781660670338

Published by Batch of Books.

Interior design and cover design by Dena McMurdie.

Cover art by virinaflora and MisterElements.

First printing, January 2020.

Table of Contents

How to Use This Book:

1. Find the category that interests you most.
2. Find a story starter that kicks your imagination into high gear.
3. Decide what should happen next and how your story will end.
4. Start writing!

Remember, it's your story. You can change anything you want. You can make your character an animal or an alien or a girl or a boy. You can add extra characters, change the setting, or switch up the point of view. Use your imagination and make the story your own!

Questions to ask yourself before you start writing:

1. What happens next in the story? You've been given a start, now it's up to you to make it a fantastic story.
2. What is your character working toward? For example, are they going on a quest, trying to survive, or navigating a friendship? Decide what your character's goal is before you start writing. This will make it easier to write your story.
3. What happens in the middle of the story?
4. How does the story end?

This morning, I woke up as a bird.

_____

_____

_____

_____

_____

_____

_____

_____

_____

_____

_____

_____

_____

_____

_____

Pop! I turned into a cookie.

_____

_____

_____

_____

_____

_____

_____

_____

_____

_____

_____

_____

_____

_____

_____

_____

_____

A wicked witch turned me into a mouse.

_____

_____

_____

_____

_____

_____

_____

_____

_____

_____

_____

_____

_____

_____

_____

_____

I shrank to the size of an ant.

A magic potion made me grow as tall as a house.

When I got to
school, my teacher
was a llama.

_____

_____

_____

_____

_____

_____

_____

_____

_____

_____

_____

_____

_____

_____

_____

I turned into a
pop star.

_____

_____

_____

_____

_____

_____

_____

_____

_____

_____

_____

_____

_____

_____

_____

My scooter turned into a monster truck.

I traded places
with a rodeo
cowgirl.

_____

_____

_____

_____

_____

_____

_____

_____

_____

_____

_____

_____

_____

I traded places with a knight.

I turned into a mermaid.

_____

_____

_____

_____

_____

_____

_____

_____

_____

_____

_____

_____

_____

_____

_____

_____

_____

ANIMALS ACTING STRANGE

My dog learned how to talk.

_____

_____

_____

_____

_____

_____

_____

_____

_____

_____

_____

_____

_____

_____

_____

My cat is secretly a superhero.

The pig was driving a car.

_____

_____

_____

_____

_____

_____

_____

_____

_____

_____

_____

_____

_____

_____

I found a monkey in my kitchen.

My best friend is a dragon.

_____

_____

_____

_____

_____

_____

_____

_____

_____

_____

_____

_____

_____

_____

All the zoo animals were out of their cages.

The unicorn jumped over the moon.

The dog could not
find the bone he
had buried.

When I got on the
carousel, my horse
came to life.

_____

_____

_____

_____

_____

_____

_____

_____

_____

_____

_____

_____

_____

_____

_____

My cat joined a
band.

_____
_____

_____
_____
_____
_____
_____
_____
_____
_____
_____
_____
_____
_____
_____

There is a dinosaur in my backyard.

_____

_____

_____

_____

_____

_____

_____

_____

_____

_____

_____

_____

_____

The bear loved wearing sunglasses.

The pig was riding a skateboard.

The hamster was
very excited.

The bird was chewing bubble gum.

My llama likes to party.

_____

_____

_____

_____

_____

_____

_____

_____

_____

_____

_____

_____

_____

_____

_____

_____

_____

_____

Today, I met a friendly dragon.

The rabbit did not come out of the hat.

The shark was surfing.

The duck was
using an umbrella
as a boat.

The chicken was riding a bicycle.

_____

_____

_____

_____

_____

_____

_____

_____

_____

_____

_____

_____

_____

_____

My cats love
taking selfies.

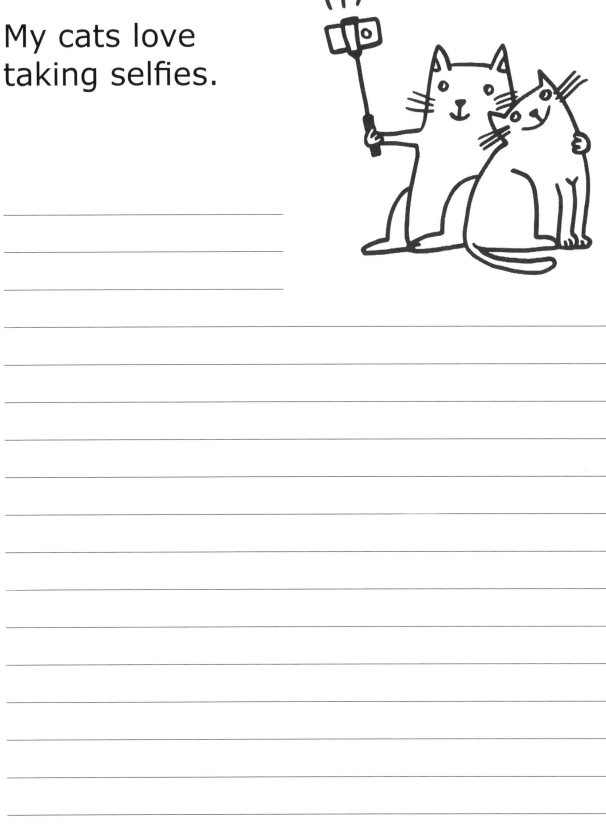

The dog wanted to be an astronaut.

_____

_____

_____

_____

_____

_____

_____

_____

_____

_____

_____

_____

_____

_____

_____

The alligator was afraid of deep water.

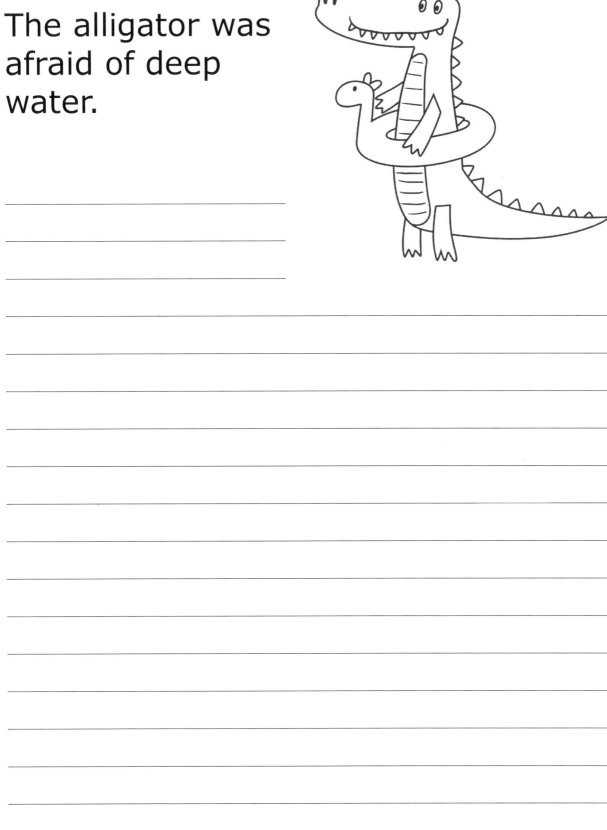

The cat was sunbathing on the beach.

The rabbit wanted to become a rock star.

_____

_____

_____

_____

_____

_____

_____

_____

_____

_____

_____

_____

_____

_____

My pet fox was
secretly a bandit.

_____

_____

_____

_____

_____

_____

_____

_____

_____

_____

_____

_____

_____

_____

_____

The dog was eating a hamburger.

The squirrel was very angry.

_____

_____

_____

_____

_____

_____

_____

_____

_____

_____

_____

_____

_____

The penguin threw the snowball.

Monsters Aliens & Other Spooky Stuff

When I looked
in the mirror, a
ghost looked back
at me.

_____

_____

_____

_____

_____

_____

_____

_____

_____

_____

_____

_____

_____

_____

My sister was a vampire.

The spaceship landed in front of me.

_____

_____

_____

_____

_____

_____

_____

_____

_____

_____

_____

_____

_____

_____

The monster stopped in my backyard.

_____

_____

_____

_____

_____

_____

_____

_____

_____

_____

_____

_____

_____

_____

_____

_____

The alien was eating an ice cream cone.

A noise woke me up in the middle of the night.

The school bus was full of monsters.

_____

_____

_____

_____

_____

_____

_____

_____

_____

_____

_____

_____

_____

The monster was reading a book.

_____

_____

_____

_____

_____

_____

_____

_____

_____

_____

_____

_____

_____

_____

A monster was in my closet.

_____

_____

_____

_____

_____

_____

_____

_____

_____

_____

_____

_____

_____

_____

My neighbor was a werewolf.

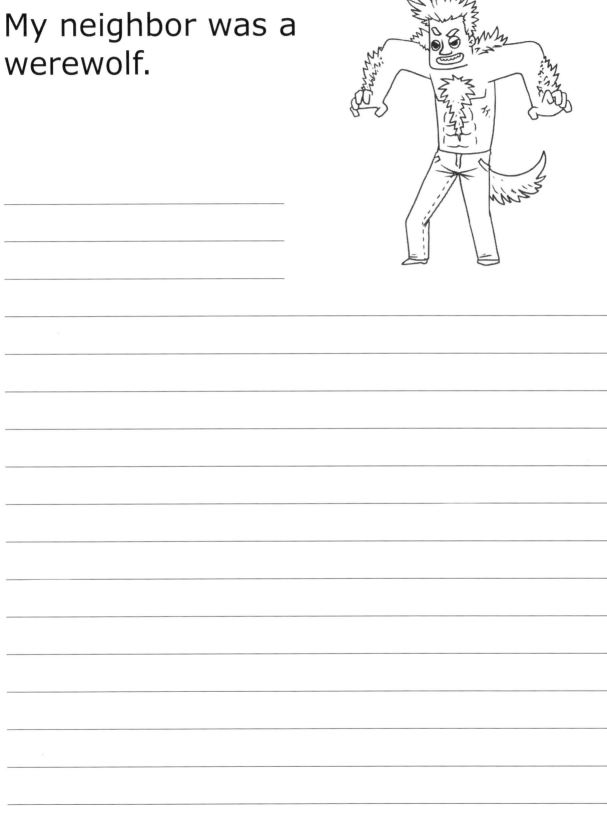

_____

_____

_____

_____

_____

_____

_____

_____

_____

_____

_____

_____

_____

_____

_____

_____

_____

An alien came to my birthday party.

_____

_____

_____

_____

_____

_____

_____

_____

_____

_____

_____

_____

_____

The vampire was bobbing for apples.

I went into the
haunted house.

_____
_____
_____

_____
_____
_____
_____
_____
_____
_____
_____
_____
_____
_____
_____
_____
_____

The monster
wanted a hug.

_____

_____

_____

_____

_____

_____

_____

_____

_____

_____

_____

_____

_____

_____

Adventure

I was kidnapped by pirates.

_____

_____

_____

_____

_____

_____

_____

_____

_____

_____

_____

_____

_____

The balloons lifted me up, up, and away.

_____

_____

_____

_____

_____

_____

_____

_____

_____

_____

_____

_____

_____

When I woke up, everyone was gone.

My toys came to life.

_____

_____

_____

_____

_____

_____

_____

_____

_____

_____

_____

_____

_____

_____

_____

A robot followed me home.

_____

_____

_____

_____

_____

_____

_____

_____

_____

_____

_____

_____

_____

_____

I found a time machine in my basement.

_____

_____

_____

_____

_____

_____

_____

_____

_____

_____

_____

_____

_____

_____

A baby dragon hatched from the egg.

_____

_____

_____

_____

_____

_____

_____

_____

_____

_____

_____

_____

_____

I saw a fairy in
the flower garden.

I was reading
a book and got
sucked into the
story.

I have magical
powers. I am a
wizard!

_____

_____

_____

_____

_____

_____

_____

_____

_____

_____

_____

_____

_____

I got zapped by a computer. Now, I am the smartest person on Earth.

_____

_____

_____

_____

_____

_____

_____

_____

_____

_____

_____

_____

_____

_____

When I rubbed an old oil lamp, a genie appeared.

_____

_____

_____

_____

_____

_____

_____

_____

_____

_____

_____

_____

_____

_____

I swung higher and higher until...

I got sucked into a video game!

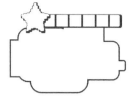
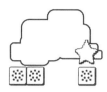

_____

_____

_____

_____

_____

_____

_____

_____

_____

_____

_____

_____

_____

_____

The submarine dove under water.

_____

_____

_____

_____

_____

_____

_____

_____

_____

_____

_____

_____

_____

I live in a giant mushroom.

_____

_____

_____

_____

_____

_____

_____

_____

_____

_____

_____

_____

_____

_____

I time-traveled back to the Old West.

_____

_____

_____

_____

_____

_____

_____

_____

_____

_____

_____

_____

_____

_____

I joined the circus.

_____

_____

_____

_____

_____

_____

_____

_____

_____

_____

_____

_____

_____

When I woke up, everything was made of candy.

_____

_____

_____

_____

_____

_____

_____

_____

_____

_____

_____

_____

I drew a picture
and it came to
life.

_____

_____

_____

_____

_____

_____

_____

_____

_____

_____

_____

_____

_____

_____

I went scuba diving in the ocean.

_____

_____

_____

_____

_____

_____

_____

_____

_____

_____

_____

_____

_____

_____

_____

I found a pair of magic shoes.

_____

_____

_____

_____

_____

_____

_____

_____

_____

_____

_____

_____

_____

_____

_____

I planted some
magic flowers in
my backyard.

_____

_____

_____

_____

_____

_____

_____

_____

_____

_____

_____

_____

_____

_____

Today, I ate a magic cupcake.

Today, I farted the
biggest fart of my
life.

_____

_____

_____

_____

_____

_____

_____

_____

_____

_____

_____

_____

_____

_____

_____

My baby sister
is actually a tiny
superhero.

The frog and the
cat had a burping
contest.

BURP!

_____

_____

_____

_____

_____

_____

_____

_____

_____

_____

_____

_____

_____

_____

Everything I touch turns to candy.

_____

_____

_____

_____

_____

_____

_____

_____

_____

_____

_____

_____

_____

_____

_____

My grandma is
a world-famous
surfer.

I am secretly a ninja.

_____

_____

_____

_____

_____

_____

_____

_____

_____

_____

_____

_____

_____

I spent the whole
day upside down.

_____

_____

_____

_____

_____

_____

_____

_____

_____

_____

_____

_____

_____

_____

My breakfast started talking to me.

_____

_____

_____

_____

_____

_____

_____

_____

_____

_____

_____

_____

_____

_____

_____

Today, I stepped in unicorn poop.

_____

_____

_____

_____

_____

_____

_____

_____

_____

_____

_____

_____

_____

_____

_____

I can fly!

_____

_____

_____

_____

_____

_____

_____

_____

_____

_____

_____

_____

_____

_____

_____

The trash was extra stinky.

_____

_____

_____

_____

_____

_____

_____

_____

_____

_____

_____

_____

_____

Ever since my cat
bit me, I can only
talk in meows
and purrs.

Meow!

Realistic Stuff

I joined the football team.

_____

_____

_____

_____

_____

_____

_____

_____

_____

_____

_____

_____

_____

I found a lost dog
on my front porch.

I dreamed I was a famous soccer player.

My family went camping in the woods.

_____

_____

_____

_____

_____

_____

_____

_____

_____

_____

_____

_____

_____

I made a wish on a shooting star.

_____
_____
_____

_____
_____
_____
_____
_____
_____
_____
_____
_____
_____
_____
_____

I went fishing with my cat.

_____

_____

_____

_____

_____

_____

_____

_____

_____

_____

_____

_____

_____

_____

I am having a
bake sale!

The ballerina was excited.

I saw everything from my treehouse.

I got into a snowball fight.

About Batch of Books

Batch of Books is a blog dedicated to finding great books for children and teens. It features reading lists, giveaways, freebies, quizzes, and other fun content.

Visit us online at www.batchofbooks.com.

If you enjoyed this book, please leave a review on Amazon.com.

Don't miss these other fun books!

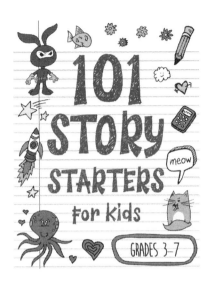

101 Story Starters for Kids
Grades 3-7
Keep your creativity going with this set of fun and exciting story starters for big kids! With longer prompts and plenty of topics to choose from, you'll be writing amazing stories in no time.

Draw Your Own Comics! Blank Comic Book
Do you love writing and drawing your own comics and graphic novels? This blank comic book offers 50 unique panel layouts for you to experiment with. You'll even find some tips and tricks in the back of the book to help you make your comic amazing!

Visit

BATCH OF BOOKS

batchofbooks.com

Picture Credits:

Made in the USA
Monee, IL
18 May 2023

34026093R00068